621 DIGITAL PRESENTS TONY ESCO

FELONIES THE NEW JIM CROW

OVERCOMING PROCRASTINATION

COULD FELONIES BE THE NEW JIM CROW BY TONY ESCO

1. INTRODUCTION: THE SETUP
2. CHAPTER 1: THE STREETS DON'T LIE
3. CHAPTER 2: HISTORY REPEATS ITSELF
4. CHAPTER 3: THE SYSTEM'S SET UP
5. CHAPTER 4: IT'S BIGGER THAN HIP-HOP
6. CHAPTER 5: FLIPPING THE SCRIPT
7. CHAPTER 6: KNOWLEDGE IS POWER
8. CHAPTER 7: THE COME UP
9. CHAPTER 8: THE NEW REVOLUTION
10. CONCLUSION: KEEP IT 100

The book takes readers on a journey from understanding the problem of felony convictions as a modern form of systemic oppression, through strategies for personal success, to a call for collective action and societal change. It maintains a raw, authentic voice throughout, blending street wisdom with factual information and practical advice.

The conclusion wraps up the book's main themes, emphasizing resilience, continuous learning, success as a form of resistance, community support, and the potential for systemic change. It ends with a powerful call to action, encouraging readers to see themselves as part of a larger movement for justice and equality.

Could Felonies Be the New Jim Crow

By Tony Esco

Introduction: The Setup

Yo, listen up. This ain't no bedtime story, and I ain't here to sugarcoat shit for you. The name's Tony Esco, and I'm about to take you on a journey through the concrete jungle where dreams get crushed faster than a beer can under a boot.

We're diving deep into a world where catching a felony can fuck up your life worse than any bullet. This book right here? It's a wake-up call, a survival guide, and a middle finger to the system all rolled into one.

From the projects to the penthouses, we're gonna break down how society's been playing us. Jim Crow might be dead, but his ghost is still haunting our asses in the form of felony convictions. It's a new game with the same old rules: keep us down, keep us out, and keep us fighting each other instead of the real enemy.

But check it – this ain't just about pointing fingers. Nah, we're here to flip the script, to show you how to navigate this minefield they call the justice system. We're gonna talk about survival, sure, but more than that, we're gonna talk about thriving. 'Cause staying alive ain't enough when you're living in a world that treats you like you're already dead.

So strap in, keep your eyes open, and your mind sharper than a razor. By the time we're done, you'll know how to spot the traps, sidestep the bullshit, and maybe, just maybe, change the game for good.

This is "Could Felonies Be the New Jim Crow." Let's get it.

Chapter 1: The Streets Don't Lie

A'ight, let's kick this off where it all begins – the streets. These concrete jungles got stories to tell, and if you listen close, you'll hear the truth louder than any courtroom gavel.

First things first, let's break down what we're dealing with. A felony ain't just some legal mumbo jumbo. In the real world, it's a brand, a scarlet letter that marks you for life. It's the difference between a future and a fuck-up, between making moves and being stuck in park.

Now, I ain't just pulling this out my ass. Let's look at the numbers, 'cause numbers don't lie even when everyone else does:

- One in three black men can expect to go to prison in their lifetime. One in three. Let that sink in.
- Felony convictions have grown like weeds. In 1980, 5% of the population had a felony record. By 2010? That shit nearly tripled to 14%.
- And guess who's catching the most heat? You already know. Black folks are locked up at five times the rate of white folks.

But these ain't just numbers on a page. These are lives, families, whole communities getting torn apart. And for what? Often for some bullshit that wouldn't even make the evening news in a white neighborhood.

Let me break it down with a real story. My boy Marcus – smart kid, good with computers. Got caught with a couple ounces of weed. Not dealing, just had it on him. Boom – felony possession. Just like that, his dreams of going to college, getting into tech? Gone. Doors slamming in his face faster than he could knock.

Compare that to Brad from the suburbs. Caught with the same amount, but his daddy knew a guy who knew a guy. Brad got community service and a stern talking-to. Now he's working at some startup, probably got stock options and shit.

The streets see this. The streets know. It ain't about justice – it's about control. It's about keeping certain folks in their place. And that place? It ain't at the top.

But here's the kicker – the streets also know how to survive. How to adapt. How to find the cracks in the system and slip through. That's what this book is about. 'Cause once you see the game for what it is, you can start playing it your way.

Next chapter, we're gonna dive into how this shit ain't new. The players might've changed, but the game? That's been rigged from the start.

Chapter 2: History Repeats Itself

A'ight, class is in session, and today we're taking a trip down memory lane. But this ain't your grandma's history lesson. We're gonna connect the dots between the past and the present, and trust me, the picture it paints ain't pretty.

Let's start with Jim Crow. For those who slept through history class, Jim Crow was a set of laws that kept black folks "separate but equal" after slavery ended. Spoiler alert: there wasn't nothing equal about it.

Jim Crow was all about:

1. Keeping us out of white spaces

2. Denying us opportunities

3. Making sure we couldn't build wealth or power

Sound familiar? That's 'cause the game ain't changed, just the rules.

Now let's look at how felonies play the same dirty game:

1. Keeping us out:
- Jim Crow had "whites only" signs. Today? We got background checks.
- Can't live in certain neighborhoods with a record. Can't even visit some countries.

2. Denying opportunities:
- Back then, they had literacy tests for voting. Now? Felony disenfranchisement.
- Jim Crow kept us out of good schools. A felony keeps you out of college financial aid.

3. Blocking wealth and power:
- They used to straight up block us from certain jobs. Now they just ask, "Have you ever been convicted of a felony?"
- Red-lining kept us out of good neighborhoods. Try getting a lease with an F on your record.

But here's the million-dollar question: Why they so scared? Why go through all this trouble to keep us down?

'Cause they know what we're capable of. They've seen what happens when we get a real shot. We don't just play the game, we change it. We innovate, we create, we lead.

Every time black folks have gotten a taste of freedom, we've excelled:

- After the Civil War? We had black senators, successful businesses, thriving communities.

- During the Harlem Renaissance? We revolutionized art, music, and literature.

- Civil Rights Movement? We changed the whole damn country.

That's why they're always trying to move the goalposts. Jim Crow, the War on Drugs, mass incarceration – it's all the same game with different names.

But here's the thing they don't want you to know: We've beaten their system before, and we can do it again. It starts with recognizing the trap. Once you see it, you can sidestep it, or better yet, dismantle it.

Next up, we're gonna break down exactly how this system is set up to trip us up at every turn. Knowledge is power, and we're about to get real powerful.

Chapter 3: The System's Set Up

Now that we've seen how history keeps trying to repeat itself, let's zoom in on how this system is designed to keep us boxed in. This chapter ain't just about pointing out problems – it's about understanding the game so we can beat it.

Let's break it down into three main areas where a felony hits you hardest:

1. Housing: Trying to Find a Crib with an F on Your Record

Picture this: You've done your time, you're ready to start fresh, but everywhere you turn, doors are slamming in your face. Why? 'Cause that box you had to check on the application might as well say "No Home for You."

- Public Housing? Forget about it. Most have blanket bans on people with felonies.
- Private rentals? Landlords can and will discriminate. They'll say it's about "safety," but we know it's about keeping certain folks out.
- Buying a home? Good luck getting a mortgage with a record. They'll look at you like you're trying to rob the bank instead of borrow from it.

Real talk: Without a stable place to live, everything else falls apart. How you supposed to keep a job, raise your kids, or stay out of trouble when you don't even know where you're sleeping next week?

2. Jobs: When Your Past Cock-Blocks Your Future

Getting that paper is hard enough, but with a felony? It's like trying to win a race with your legs tied together.

- Most applications have that dreaded box: "Have you ever been convicted of a felony?" Check yes, and watch your resume hit the trash.
- Licenses for everything from cutting hair to driving a taxi? Many got restrictions for felons.
- Corporate jobs? They'll talk about "company culture" and "liability," but what they mean is they don't want you there.

And it's not just about getting a job – it's about building a career. With a felony, you're often stuck in dead-end gigs, watching everyone else climb the ladder while you're glued to the bottom rung.

3. Education: They Don't Want Us Learning, They Want Us Burning

Knowledge is power, and they know it. That's why they make it so damn hard for felons to get an education.

- Federal student aid? Not if you've got drug charges. They'd rather see you slinging on the corner than studying in a classroom.
- Many colleges ask about criminal history. They say it's not an automatic disqualifier, but we know how that game is played.
- Vocational programs, especially in fields like healthcare or education? Often closed to people with records.

Without education, we're cut off from better jobs, higher earnings, and the kind of knowledge that lets us challenge the system.

But here's the thing: This setup isn't just screwing with individuals. It's messing up whole communities. When you can't get housing, jobs, or education, what options are left? For too many, it's back to the streets, back to the hustle, back to the cycle that got them caught up in the first place.

This system isn't broken – it's working exactly how they designed it. It's set up to keep certain folks down, to make sure that even after you've "paid your debt to society," you're still paying interest.

But every system has its weaknesses. In the next chapter, we're gonna talk about how this shit affects more than just the person with the record. 'Cause when they come for one of us, they come for all of us.

Facts!

Chapter 4: It's Bigger Than Hip-Hop

A'ight, now we're getting to the heart of it. This chapter's about understanding that when the system puts its boot on one neck, the whole body feels it. This felony shit? It's not just about the person catching the case. It's about families, neighborhoods, whole generations getting caught in the crossfire.

Let's break it down:

The Family Fallout

When one person gets hit with a felony, the shockwaves hit everyone around them:

- Mommas and Pops: They're left picking up the pieces. Paying for lawyers, holding down the fort, trying to keep the family together when the system's trying to tear it apart.
- Kids: Growing up with a parent behind bars or struggling to get by with a record? That shit leaves scars. We're talking about higher rates of depression, anxiety, acting out in school. The system's not just punishing the parent; it's setting up the next generation for failure.
- Partners: Imagine trying to build a life with someone who can't get a job, can't rent an apartment, can't even vote. It puts strain on relationships, breaks up families.

The Community Collapse

A neighborhood ain't just a bunch of houses. It's a network, an ecosystem. And when too many people in that ecosystem are marked with felonies, the whole thing starts to fall apart:

- Economic Impact: When a big chunk of your workforce can't get decent jobs, the whole community suffers. Businesses don't open, property values drop, and the cycle of poverty digs in deeper.
- Social Breakdown: Trust erodes. If everyone's either been through the system or knows someone who has, how you gonna trust the cops, the schools, any institution?
- Political Powerlessness: In some states, felons lose their right to vote. Entire communities lose their political voice, making it even harder to change the system that's oppressing them.

The Cultural Consequence

This ain't just about economics and politics. It's about our very culture:

- Role Models: When the visible success stories in a community are either athletes, entertainers, or hustlers, what message does that send to the youth?
- Normalization: In some neighborhoods, going to prison is seen as a rite of passage. Not because our people are inherently criminal, but because the system has made it so damn common.
- Perpetual Punishment: Even after time is served, the stigma remains. It seeps into every aspect of life, changing how people see themselves and how the world sees them.

The Ripple Effect

Here's where it gets really fucked up. This isn't a one-generation problem. The effects of mass incarceration and felony stigma ripple out across time:

- Generational Wealth: When you can't get a good job, can't own a home, can't get an education, you can't build wealth. And when you can't build wealth, you can't pass anything down to your kids. The system ensures that poverty becomes a family tradition.
- Cycle of Incarceration: Kids with incarcerated parents are more likely to end up in the system themselves. It's not because crime is in their DNA; it's because the deck is stacked against them from day one.
- Community Brain Drain: When the brightest minds in a community are either locked up or locked out of opportunities, who's left to lead? Who's there to innovate, to create businesses, to teach the next generation?

Now, I know this chapter's been heavy. It's supposed to be. Because understanding the full weight of this problem is the first step to lifting it.

But don't get it twisted – this ain't a pity party. This is about recognizing the full scope of what we're up against. Because once you see how deep this runs, you understand why surface-level solutions ain't gonna cut it.

In the next chapter, we're gonna start talking about how to flip this script. Because knowing the problem is only half the battle. The other half? That's about taking action, about changing the game from the inside out.

Remember, they might have written the rules, but that doesn't mean we can't learn to beat them at their own game. Stay tuned.

Chapter 5: Flipping the Script

Listen up, 'cause this is where shit gets real. We've talked about the problem, now let's talk solutions. It's time to flip the script, to take this game they've rigged against us and turn it on its head.

Changing the Laws

First things first, we gotta attack this shit at the source:

1. Ban the Box: We need to push for laws that remove that felony question from job applications. Let a brother get his foot in the door before they start judging.

2. Expungement Reform: Make it easier to clear your record. If you've done your time and stayed clean, you should get a real second chance.

3. Voting Rights: Felons who've served their time should get their voting rights back, no questions asked. We can't change the system if we can't vote.

4. Sentencing Reform: Push for alternatives to incarceration. Drug treatment instead of jail time. Community service instead of fines we can't pay.

Even Jesus Was a Felon

Pray 4 Forgiveness

Programs That Give a Second Shot

It ain't just about changing laws. We need programs that actually help people get back on their feet:

1. Job Training: Not that weak-ass "here's how to write a resume" shit. Real training for real jobs that pay.

2. Education Behind Bars: If you're gonna lock someone up, at least give them a chance to come out smarter than they went in.

3. Transitional Housing: Safe, stable housing for people just getting out. Can't expect someone to stay straight if they're sleeping on the streets.

4. Mental Health and Addiction Services: A lot of brothers are self-medicating for trauma. Let's treat the cause, not just the symptoms.

Hustle the Right Way

Now, for my people out there trying to stay clean and still eat, listen up:

1. Entrepreneurship: Can't get a job? Make your own. Start small, think big. From selling water on the corner to owning the whole damn block.

2. Tech Skills: The digital hustle is real. Learn to code, do graphic design, anything that lets you work without someone checking your background.

3. Trade Skills: Plumbers, electricians, mechanics – these jobs pay, and a lot of them don't trip about your past.

4. Network: Find mentors who've been where you are. Join groups for formerly incarcerated entrepreneurs. Your network is your net worth.

Become A YOUTUBER

Remember, flipping the script ain't just about you. It's about creating a blueprint for the next generation. Every move you make, every success you have, is a middle finger to the system that tried to write you off.

In the next chapter, we're gonna talk about arming yourself with knowledge. 'Cause in this war, information is the most powerful weapon you can have.

Chapter 6: Knowledge is Power

A'ight, class is in session again. But this time, we're not just learning about the problem – we're learning how to solve it. Knowledge is power, and in this chapter, we're about to get real powerful.

Educating the Youth

The best way to beat the system? Never get caught up in it in the first place. Here's how we educate our young'uns

1. Know Your Rights: Teach kids how to interact with cops. What to say, what not to say, and when to shut the hell up and ask for a lawyer.

2. Financial Literacy: School doesn't teach you how to manage money. We need to. Budgeting, saving, investing – this is the shit that keeps you off the corner.

3. Real History: Not that watered-down textbook crap. Teach them about the Black Panthers, about Malcolm, about the real freedom fighters.

4. Critical Thinking: Teach kids to question everything. Why are things the way they are? Who benefits? How can we change it?

Understanding Your Rights

When the law comes knocking, you better know how to answer:

1. Miranda Rights: "You have the right to remain silent" ain't just something cops say on TV. Know what it means and use it.

2. Search and Seizure: Know when cops can and can't search you, your car, or your crib. Don't consent to shit unless they got a warrant.

3. Plea Bargains: Understand what you're agreeing to. A plea might seem like the easy way out, but it can fuck up your life long-term.

4. Expungement and Sealing: Know the difference and know if you qualify. This could be your ticket to a clean slate.

Building a Support System

You can't do this shit alone. Here's how to build a crew that'll have your back:

1. Find Your People: Look for organizations that support formerly incarcerated folks. They've been where you are, they know the struggle.

2. Legal Aid: Know where to find free or low-cost legal help. A good lawyer can be the difference between freedom and a cage.

3. Mentorship: Find someone who's walked your path and made it out. Learn from their wins and their losses.

4. Community Organizations: Get involved in your hood. Tenant associations, community gardens, youth programs – this is how you build power from the ground up.

Continued Learning

The game is always changing, so you gotta stay sharp:

1. Know the Laws: Keep up with changes in criminal justice reform. What worked yesterday might not work today.

2. Technology: The digital divide is real. Bridge that gap. Learn how to use computers, smartphones, social media – these are tools for success.

3. Your Rights as a Returning Citizen: Know what opportunities are available to you. Job training programs, housing assistance, education grants – there's help out there if you know where to look.

4. Political Education: Understand how the system works so you can work the system. Know who your representatives are and hold them accountable.

Remember, knowledge ain't just about books and classrooms. It's about street smarts meets book smarts. It's about taking everything you've learned the hard way and using it to make a better way.

In the next chapter, we're gonna talk about success stories. 'Cause you need to know that it's possible to beat this game, no matter how rigged it seems.

Felons Who Changed There Lives

BG
Soulja Blacc
Boogs
Lucky
Illwee
Lump
Moose

Chapter 7: The Come Up

Now we're getting to the good part. This chapter is all about the come up – how to turn your pain into your gain, how to build an empire from the bottom up. We're gonna look at some real success stories, brothers and sisters who've been where you are and made it to the other side.

From Cell Block to Corner Office

Let me tell you about Marcus. Dude caught a felony for some bullshit drug charge when he was 19. Did three years, came out with nothing but the clothes on his back and a fire in his belly. Here's how he flipped it:

1. Education: Marcus hit the books hard in prison. Came out with a GED and started taking community college classes the day he got out.

2. Hustle: Couldn't get a regular job, so he started detailing cars. Built a clientele, saved every penny.

3. Network: Got involved with a re-entry program. Met mentors, other ex-cons who'd made it. Learned from their playbook.

4. Entrepreneurship: Took his car detailing hustle and turned it into a full-service auto shop. Now he's employing other brothers with records, giving them the chance he wished he had.

The lesson? Your past doesn't define your future. It's fuel for your fire.

Tech Revolution

Next up, we got Shanice. Sister caught a case for check fraud, did 18 months. But peep game on how she turned it around:

1. Skill Building: Learned to code while inside. Came out a self-taught web developer.

2. Freelancing: Started small, building websites for local businesses. Built a reputation for solid work and reliability.

3. Remote Work: Tech companies care more about your skills than your record. Found a startup willing to give her a shot based on her portfolio, not her past.

4. Giving Back: Now she runs coding bootcamps for formerly incarcerated folks. Changing the game from the inside out.

The takeaway? The digital hustle is real, and it doesn't care about your record.

Policy Changemaker

Let's talk about Jerome. Homeboy did 10 years on a drug trafficking charge. Now he's changing the laws that locked him up:

1. Education: Got his bachelor's and master's while inside. Came out with more degrees than the cops who arrested him.

2. Activism: Got involved with criminal justice reform organizations. Started speaking at rallies, writing op-eds.

3. Politics: Ran for city council on a platform of reform. Won his seat and is now pushing for changes from the inside.

4. Mentorship: Uses his position to create opportunities for other returning citizens. Internships, job programs, the whole nine.

The message? Sometimes you gotta change the system from the inside out.

Building Generational Wealth

Last but not least, we got Keisha. Sister got caught up in a fraud case, did five years. Now she's building the kind of wealth her grandkids will thank her for:

1. Financial Education: Learned everything she could about money management and investing while inside.

2. Real Estate: Started small, buying and renovating foreclosed homes in her neighborhood.

3. Community Investment: Uses her profits to fund small business loans for other ex-cons trying to get on their feet.

4. Legacy Building: Setting up trust funds for her kids' education, breaking the cycle of poverty and incarceration.

The lesson? It's not just about getting rich; it's about lifting up your whole community.

These stories ain't fairy tales. They're blueprints. Every one of these brothers and sisters started exactly where you are. They faced the same closed doors, the same skeptical looks, the same system designed to keep them down.

But they didn't just survive – they thrived. They took every "no" as motivation, every setback as a setup for a comeback. They rewrote their stories, and now they're helping others do the same.

You got the same fire in you. The same potential. The same ability to flip the script and write your own ending. In the next chapter, we're gonna talk about how to take everything you've learned and turn it into a movement. 'Cause this ain't just about changing your life – it's about changing the game for everyone.

Chapter 8: The New Revolution

A'ight, we've come a long way. We've broken down the problem, laid out the solutions, and seen what's possible when we put in that work. Now it's time to talk about the big picture.

This chapter is about starting a revolution – not with guns and bombs, but with knowledge, unity, and action.

This Ain't About Playing Victim

First things first – we ain't here to cry about how unfair life is. We know it's unfair. We've lived it. But dwelling on that shit won't change a damn thing. This revolution is about taking control, about refusing to be defined by a system that was never meant for us to succeed in.

1. Mindset Shift: Stop seeing yourself as an ex-con, a felon, whatever label they've slapped on you. You're a survivor, a hustler, a future CEO.

2. Accountability: Yeah, the system is rigged. But that doesn't mean we're powerless. Take responsibility for your choices and your future.

3. Proactive, Not Reactive: Don't wait for opportunities to come to you. Create them. See a need in your community? Fill it. See a problem? Solve it.

Changing the Game for the Next Generation

This revolution ain't just about us. It's about making sure our kids and our kids' kids don't have to fight the same battles:

1. Mentorship: Every one of us who makes it has a responsibility to reach back and pull someone else up.

2. Education Reform: Push for schools that teach real-life skills – financial literacy, entrepreneurship, civil rights.

3. Community Investment: Support businesses owned by formerly incarcerated folks. Create job opportunities. Build wealth that stays in the community.

4. Political Engagement: Vote in every election, not just the big ones. Local politics is where real change starts.

The Blueprint for Breaking the Cycle

Here's how we turn this movement into lasting change:

1. Unity: We gotta stop seeing each other as competition and start seeing each other as allies. The more of us succeed, the harder it is for them to ignore us.

2. Economic Power: Build businesses, invest in real estate, create jobs. Economic power is the key to political power.

3. Media Representation: Tell our own stories. Use social media, start podcasts, write books. Control the narrative.

4. Legal Action: Challenge unjust laws in court. Support organizations that provide legal aid to our communities.

5. Policy Change: Push for reforms at every level – local, state, federal. Ban the box, restore voting rights, end cash bail.

The New Underground Railroad

Think of this movement as the new Underground Railroad. We're not escaping physical slavery, but we're breaking free from a system of legal and economic oppression:

1. Safe Houses: Create spaces where formerly incarcerated folks can get support, resources, and community.

2. Conductors: Be a guide for others coming home. Show them the ropes, connect them with opportunities.

3. Freedom Papers: Instead of forged documents, we're talking education, certifications, business licenses – the papers that give you freedom in today's world.

4. Coded Language: Use your knowledge of the streets to navigate the corporate world. The hustle doesn't change, just the product.

LETS GO!

The Call to Action

This is where the rubber meets the road. Here's what you can do right now to be part of this revolution:

1. Educate Yourself: Keep learning, keep growing. The more you know, the more dangerous you are to the status quo.

2. Spread the Word: Share this book, share your story. The more people understand the reality of life after incarceration, the harder it is to ignore.

3. Get Involved: Join organizations fighting for criminal justice reform. Volunteer, donate, show up to meetings.

4. Build Your Empire: Whatever your hustle is, make it legit and make it grow. Your success is a form of resistance.

5. Vote: And not just for presidents. Vote in every election, especially local ones. That's where the decisions that affect our daily lives are made.

Remember, every great movement started with a few people who refused to accept things as they were. We've got the numbers, we've got the knowledge, and we've got the motivation. All we need now is to come together and make it happen.

This ain't the end of the book – it's the beginning of a movement. Let's get to work.

Conclusion: Keep It 100

We've come a long way, fam. From breaking down how felonies are the new Jim Crow to laying out a blueprint for a whole damn revolution. But now comes the hard part – taking everything we've talked about and putting it into action.

The Real Talk

Let's keep it 100 – this shit ain't gonna be easy. The system's been in place for generations, and it ain't gonna change overnight. You're gonna face setbacks, closed doors, and people who'll try to convince you that you can't win.

But here's the thing: Every time they tell you "no," every time they try to put you back in that box they've labeled "felon" or "ex-con," that's fuel for your fire. Use it. Let it drive you.

Resources for the Revolution

Knowledge is power, but knowing where to find help is straight-up survival. Here's a quick rundown of resources to get you started:

1. Legal Help:
- The Equal Justice Initiative (EJI): They provide legal representation to people who have been illegally convicted, unfairly sentenced, or abused in state jails and prisons.
- Legal Aid Society: Offers free legal services to low-income individuals.

2. Job Training and Employment:
- The Center for Employment Opportunities (CEO): Provides employment services to people with criminal convictions.
- Homeboy Industries: Offers job training and support to formerly gang-involved and previously incarcerated people.

3. Education:
- Prison Education Project: Provides education to incarcerated individuals.
- The Formerly Incarcerated College Graduates Network: Supports formerly incarcerated individuals pursuing higher education.

4. Advocacy and Policy Reform:
- The Sentencing Project: Works for a fair and effective U.S. criminal justice system by promoting reforms in sentencing policy and addressing unjust racial disparities and practices.
- Cut50: Aims to reduce the prison population while making communities safer.

5. Mental Health and Addiction Services:
- SAMHSA's National Helpline: 1-800-662-HELP (4357) - Free, confidential, 24/7 treatment referral and information service.

Remember, reaching out for help ain't weakness – it's strategy. Use these resources, build your network, and keep pushing forward.

FUCK SUICIDE

Im d'ying 2

Live

The Final Word

At the end of the day, this book ain't just about felonies or Jim Crow or any of that. It's about us. It's about our power, our potential, and our undeniable right to thrive in a world that's been trying to write us off since day one.

We've been through slavery, Jim Crow, the War on Drugs, and now this mass incarceration bullshit. But we're still here. Still fighting. Still rising. That ain't by accident. It's because we're resilient as fuck, creative as hell, and stronger together than they could ever imagine. So here's what I want you to take away from all this:

1. Your past don't define you. It's just the opening chapter in a book you're still writing.
2. Knowledge is your weapon, your shield, and your key. Never stop learning, never stop growing.
3. Success is the best revenge. Every dollar you make legally, every vote you cast, every kid you mentor is a middle finger to the system that tried to bury you.
4. You ain't alone in this fight. Reach out, link up, and build with your community. We're all we got, but we're all we need.

1. The game is rigged, but it ain't over. We can change the rules if we work together, stay focused, and refuse to give up.

Remember, every time you win, every time you beat the odds, you're not just changing your life. You're changing the narrative. You're showing the world that we ain't what they think we are. We're leaders, innovators, game-changers.

Remember, every time you win, every time you beat the odds, you're not just changing your life. You're changing the narrative. You're showing the world that we ain't what they think we are. We're leaders, innovators, game-changers.

So go out there and do your thing. Build that business. Run for office. Mentor that kid. Whatever you do, do it with purpose. Do it knowing that you're part of something bigger than yourself.
This is more than a book. It's a movement. It's a revolution. And it starts with you.
Stay strong. Stay focused. And above all, stay free.
Peace and Hair Grease,

Tony Esco

Coming Soon!

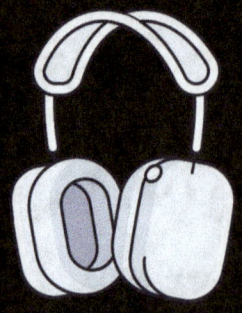

BABY
Esco

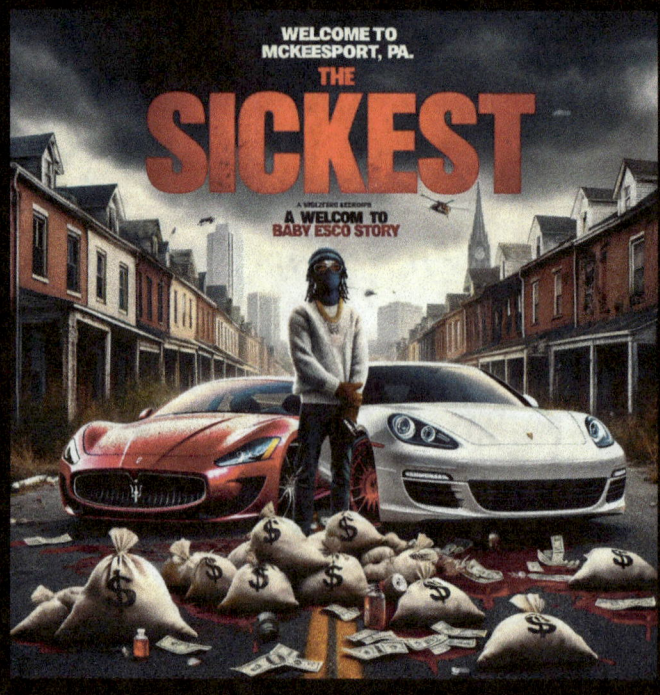

Bonus CONTENT

Obtaining a CDL and Getting into Trucking

Listen up, 'cause I'm about to put you on game to a hustle that can have you stacking paper and seeing the country at the same time. I'm talking about getting your CDL and breaking into the trucking game.

Introduction to CDL (Commercial Driver's License)

First things first, let's break down what it takes to get that CDL:

1. Get your permit: Study the CDL manual, pass a written test. It's like getting your regular license, but with more rules to remember.
2. Complete a training program: You gotta learn how to handle those big rigs.
3. Pass the skills test: Show 'em you can drive that truck like a boss.
4. Get your medical card: Gotta prove you're healthy enough to handle the road.

Now, I know what you're thinking. "But Esco, who's gonna train a felon?" I got you. There are programs out there specifically for our people:

- [CDL Training Resource] | Phone: 1-800-555-5678 These folks specialize in helping brothers and sisters with records get their CDL. They know the struggle, and they're here to help you win.

Trucking Companies Hiring Felons

Once you got that CDL in your hand, it's time to get hired. Check out these companies that are known for giving our people a second chance:

1. Swift Transportation
2. C.R. England
3. Knight Transportation
4. Schneider National

Do your research, reach out, and don't be afraid to shoot your shot. Remember, in this game, persistence pays off.

Chapter 10: Government Jobs That Accept Felons and Felony-Friendly States

Now, let me put you up on some game that might surprise you. The government, the same system that locked us up, they're actually one of the biggest employers of people with records. Let's break it down.

Federal Jobs with Felony Acceptance

1. **United States Postal Service (USPS):** They're always hiring, and they don't trip about your past as long as you're straight now.
2. **Transportation Security Administration (TSA):** Ironic, right? But they're about giving second chances.
3. **Army Corps of Engineers:** They got civilian positions that don't require a clean record.

Applying for Government Jobs

Here's how you increase your chances:

1. Be honest about your record. They're gonna find out anyway, so own it.
2. Emphasize your skills and what you've done since your conviction.
3. Get letters of recommendation. Show them you got people vouching for you.

For more info, hit up: [Government Job Resource] | Phone: 1-800-555-7890

Felony-Friendly States

Not all states are created equal when it comes to giving our people a fair shot. Here are some that are known for being more open:

1. California
2. Colorado
3. New York
4. Minnesota
5. New Jersey

Do your research before you make a move. Each state has its own rules and opportunities.

Government Jobs That Accept Felons and Felony-Friendly States

[...]

Felony-Friendly States

Not all states are created equal when it comes to giving our people a fair shot. Here are some that are known for being more open:

1. California
2. Colorado
3. New York
4. Minnesota
5. New Jersey
6. Ohio
7. Pennsylvania

Let's zoom in on Ohio and Pennsylvania, 'cause these states are stepping up their game when it comes to giving our people a second chance.

Ohio: The Buckeye State of Second Chances

Ohio's been putting in work to help folks with records get back on their feet. Here's why it's a solid spot for our people:

1. Ban the Box: Ohio removed that dreaded felony question from state job applications. They're looking at your skills, not your past.
2. Certificate of Qualification for Employment (CQE): This is like a golden ticket. It can help you get licenses, jobs, and even housing that might usually be off-limits with a record.
3. Expungement and Sealing: Ohio's been expanding who can get their records cleaned up. More offenses are eligible now, giving more of our people a fresh start.

Resources in Ohio:

- **Ohio Justice & Policy Center:** https://www.ohiojpc.org/
- **Ohio Reentry Coalition:** https://www.reentrycoalition.ohio.gov/
- **Legal Aid Society of Columbus:** https://www.columbuslegalaid.org/

Pennsylvania: The Keystone State of Redemption

Pennsylvania's been making moves to give our folks a fair shake. Here's what makes it stand out:

1. Clean Slate Law: This is big. It automatically seals certain criminal records after a period of time. You don't even have to ask for it.
2. Ban the Box: Like Ohio, Pennsylvania got rid of that felony checkbox on state job applications.
3. Fair Chance Hiring: Some cities in PA, like Philadelphia, have laws that make employers consider your qualifications before your criminal history.

1. Occupational Licensing Reform: They've been working on making it easier for people with records to get licensed for different jobs. Resources in Pennsylvania:
   - Community Legal Services of Philadelphia: https://clsphila.org/
   - Pennsylvania Reentry Council: https://www.cor.pa.gov/community-reentry/Pages/default.aspx
   - CareerLink: https://www.pacareerlink.pa.gov/

Now, don't get it twisted. These states ain't perfect, and you're still gonna face challenges. But they're at least trying to level the playing field. If you're thinking about a fresh start, these might be spots to consider.

Remember, though, laws can change, and every situation is different. Always do your own research and maybe chat with a lawyer or reentry specialist before making any big moves.

Side Hustles for Mechanics: Becoming a Street Mechanic

For my people with skills under the hood, listen up. Being a street mechanic can be your ticket to financial freedom. Here's how to get started:

How to Start a Street Mechanic Business

1. Essential tools: Start with the basics - wrenches, sockets, jacks, and stands. Build your arsenal as you grow.
2. Licensing: Check your local laws. You might need a business license or special permits.
3. Insurance: Cover your ass. Get liability insurance in case something goes wrong.

Building a Client Base

1. Start with friends and family. Word of mouth is your best friend.
2. Use social media. Post before and after pics of your work.
3. Partner with local auto parts stores. They might send customers your way.

Mechanic Job Platforms

Check out these sites for side gigs:

- YourMechanic.com
- Wrench.com
- [Mechanic Resources] | Phone: 1-800-555-6543

Remember, every car you fix is a step towards building your empire. Stay legal, stay safe, and stack that paper.

MORE BONUSES

Credit Repair Counseling from 621 Digital

A'ight, now we're getting into some real game. Your credit score? That's like your financial street cred. And just like your rep on the streets, it can be rebuilt. That's where 621 Digital comes in.

Business and Personal Credit Repair

621 Digital ain't your average credit repair joint. They specialize in helping our people - felons who are trying to get their hustle legal and their paper straight. Here's what they offer:

1. Business Credit Building: They'll show you how to separate your personal credit from your business credit. That's key for protecting your assets.
2. Personal Credit Repair: Got collections? Late payments? They know how to challenge that shit and get it cleaned up.
3. Resource Access: They got the plug on programs and opportunities specifically for people with records.

Credit Trade-In Programs

This is where it gets real interesting. 621 Digital can show you how to leverage good credit to build your business.

We're talking:
- Business credit cards
- Equipment financing
- Real estate investments

It's about using the system to build wealth, not just survive.

Contact 621 Digital

Credit Trade-In Programs
This is where it gets real interesting. 621 Digital can show you how to leverage good credit to build your business. We're talking:
- Business credit cards
- Equipment financing
- Real estate investments

It's about using the system to build wealth, not just survive.
Contact 621 Digital

Booking and Public Speaking Services

Now, let me tell you about another way to flip your story into success. Public speaking. Yeah, you heard me right. The same experiences that got you locked up? They can be your ticket to the stage.

Tony Esco's Speaking Services

That's right, I'm out here doing this myself. I'm talking in jails, churches, community centers, anywhere people need to hear the real. Here's what I'm bringing to the table:

1. **Overcoming Adversity: I break down how to turn your biggest L's into your biggest lessons.**
2. **Starting a Business After a Felony: I'm giving the blueprint on how to go from cell block to CEO.**
3. **Community Empowerment: This ain't just about individual success. It's about lifting up the whole hood.**

Booking Information

Want to bring this knowledge to your community? Here's how to reach me:

- Phone: 614-547-3286 (leave a message)
- Email: tonyesco@gmail.com
- [Book Tony Esco with 621 Digital]

Remember, your story has power. Use it to inspire, to teach, to change lives. That's how we really beat the system - by turning our pain into purpose.

REAL TALK, GRATITUDE, AND GAME

Yo, if you're still with me, I gotta salute you. Writing this book wasn't just about putting words on a page—it's about giving you the tools to hustle your way out of whatever box the system tried to put you in. I hope this book helps you flip the script and take control of your life, 'cause that's what it's all about.

Now, let me keep it a buck with you—I'm in the middle of my own war. I'm facing six felony charges 'cause some clown broke into my crib, and in that heat of the moment, I allegedly put one in his leg. Now, I'm fighting to clear my name. So, I'm asking you to send up a prayer for me. But know this—I ain't letting this be the end of my story. I'm the one writing my life, and this chapter ain't over yet.

Bonus Chapter: Securing a Crib with a Record—The Hustle

Let's talk real—finding a place to live when you've got felonies on your record is like trying to hustle in a game that's rigged against you. But I'm here to tell you, it ain't impossible. You just gotta know how to play your cards, especially when dealing with private landlords.

How to Talk to Private Landlords Like a Boss

When you step to a private landlord, you gotta come correct. Don't be on some nervous, head-down type shit—stand tall, look 'em in the eye, and show 'em you mean business. Here's the play:

- **Be Real:** Don't sugarcoat your past. Let them know you've been through some shit, but keep it short and to the point. Make it clear you're about moving forward.
- **Show Your Money:** Landlords wanna know you can pay, so come ready with proof. Flash those pay stubs, bank statements, or a letter from your job. If you've got side hustles bringing in cash, let that be known too.
- **Flip the Script:** Talk about your hustle, your steady income, and your goals. Show 'em you're on the grind and making moves in the right direction. A strong mindset can change the whole conversation.

The Power of a Positive Mindset
When you're standing in front of a landlord, they ain't just judging your past—they're judging your whole vibe. Show them you're responsible, got your head on straight, and you're not the same person who caught those charges. Confidence is everything.

More Game on Housing

- **HUD Programs:** Don't sleep on government help. HUD's got housing programs that can hook you up.
- **Reentry Programs:** There are programs out there designed to help people like us get back on our feet. Tap into those resources.
- **Transitional Housing:** Some states got spots for people trying to get their life back on track. Use 'em if you need to.
- **Build Connections:** Sometimes it's not what you know but who you know. Make those connections count.

Final Words of Hustle and Faith

We all got a past, but that don't define who we are. Even Jesus and his crew had warrants, and they didn't let that stop them from handling business. Same goes for us. Jesus said, "With God, all things are possible," and Muhammad reminded us, "The strongest of you is not the one who overpowers others, but the one who controls themselves when angry." That's some real talk. No matter what you're facing, never back down. Keep grinding, keep pushing, and know you got the strength to rise above it all.

Thanks for rolling with me through this book. Let's keep building, keep hustling, and show the world we're stronger than anything they throw at us. We're in this together, and we're gonna win.

Special Dedication

This one's for my mom, Joyce Quarles. Even though you're not here, your son is still grinding, staying strong, and moving with the strength you instilled in me. You taught me never to say "I can't," and trust me, I remember those whoopings when I did, lol. You laid the foundation for me to live by three things: God, Family, and Success.

A special shoutout to my Grandma—always holding me down and giving me the strength to never back down. You've been my rock, and I carry that with me every day.

And to my dad, Cool Frank, thank you for instilling that relentless work ethic in me. You showed me how to hustle.

Aunt Sonya, you always believed in me, always knew I was destined for greatness. You saw the GOAT in me before I even did. Love y'all to the fullest. This book is for you.

Rest In Power

Marva Rudolph

CooL "THE G.O.A.T" Frank

Hazelwood Legend

Greatest of all time

Sonya Rudolph
Aunty

www.ingramcontent.com/pod-product-compliance
Lightning Source LLC
Chambersburg PA
CBHW071837210526
45479CB00001B/174